Whispers of a Widow

Jeannie McCullough

For my beloved David.

THE ABYSS

I screamed into the abyss.
Opened my mouth wide and screamed.
Eyes closed tight.
The abyss enveloped me.
When my eyes opened I saw race helmets, hockey helmets,
photos and left over memories.
They did not comfort me. They reminded me of what I lost.
They were blank.
They were empty.
They meant nothing.
I screamed louder.
The heart pain real.
The pain meant more to me than the loss.
He left me with a memory of love in the kitchen and hands held
in the night.
No more passion.
No more fire.
Only a deep burning ember to warm the night.
The love of old men and the longing of a woman.
The love of a lifetime.
The love of lovers and those who mourn.
I screamed again yet no one answered.
But I knew he heard.
And he held out his hand in the night.
And the abyss was no more.

CAN'T SLEEP

Stillness
Silence
Can't sleep

Look at notes
Play music
Reread texts

Decaf coffee
Pet the dog
Tell her he loved her too

Make a list
Turn up heat
Cuddle blanket

Think of him
Start to grin
Numbness never ends

Table of Contents

EVERY MORNING STARTS THE SAME

Every morning starts the same
Every night the sad refrain
See your faces
See your fears
Breaking hearts
Drying tears

A losers love that cannot give
Rejected hearts desire to live
Silent scream unnoticed now
All we gave we lost somehow

Every morning starts the same
Every night the sad refrain
See your faces
See your fears
Breaking hearts
Drying tears

Years of love and sacrifice
Deep resentment pays the price
Someone pierced by sharpened lance
Someone begs another chance

No more giggles
Youth is gone
Crazy straws and silly songs
Home is nowhere to be found
Children left a hollow sound

Every morning starts the same
Every night the sad refrain
See your faces
See your fears
Heart is breaking
Drying tears

WHISPERS OF A WIDOW

Whispers of a widow.
Catch them they say.
Don't let your musings
All blow away.

Write what you're feeling.
Write now then read.
Words come a howling at hurricane speed.

Wake to a new day,
They all slip away.
Silent, I'm waiting for something to say.

Mornings, I sit where the shadows are long.
Rocking my chair as the birds sing their song,
New light is only a sunrise away.
Whispers a widow with nothing to say.

Words of a widow,
Whisper them now.
Sunset is coming.
And darkness will shroud
All that you long for,
All that you pray.
Whispers a widow with so much to say.

NOT THE FALLIN APART TYPE

They ask me how'm I doin?
I say I'm doin fine. But in their eyes a question. So, I feel the need to add something for them. So I say, "I guess I'm not the fallin apart type. But I sure do miss him."

I miss his presence, his laughter, his huge hands and soft feet. I miss his calm and his quiet when things weren't going well. I miss his genuine love and the sadness in his eyes. He could reach things I can't and carry things I can't and move things I won't. He could fix things I can't and manage three remotes and know when to change the oil. He could watch Denzel or Hallmark on any given day. I miss a bustling house full of chatter and movement and the opening and closing of doors.

But I'm fine. I'm not the fallin apart type. But I sure do miss him.

MY HUSBAND SLURPED HIS COFFEE

My husband slurped his coffee
And blew his nose too loud
He liked to dress as SpongeBob
And cut up for a crowd.

An egg was never safe
With David and his knife.
He'd cut it till it ran the rim and fled its very life.

And often when he talked of love, a race car came to mind.
He'd run to all the checkered flags
On any track he'd find.

But now my goofy husband has gone and I'm alone.
And all those silly memories become what feels like home.

My coffee time is quiet
My eggs are safe and sound.
No nose is blown with vigor
The house is without sound.

So here I sit in quiet
My pinky lifted high.
I sip my coffee quietly
And all alone I cry.

My David was the funny one
The light that lit the room
He made each day a memory
Then left us way too soon.

So when you think of David
Remember to stop by.
We'll reminisce on memories
And laugh until we cry.

TODAY IS JANUARY 15, 2023

It's been one month and one day since my husband died.
I will not be afraid of tomorrow nor will I drown my sorrows.
I will do the will of God as I hear it and I have heard it.
I cannot pretend I don't know the voice of Jesus for he is my shepherd and I am his sheep.

AS LONG AS YOU'RE OK

If you say goodbye I'll cry
But darling I won't die
As long as you're ok

Save my memory for a while
Yours will always make me smile
All we had and all we lost
Feel the heartache
Count the cost

If you walk away I'll cry
But darling I won't die
As long as you're ok

All of mine was all of yours
Two hearts washed on different shores
Drifting might have eased the pain
Battle lost and nothing gained

If you stay away I'll cry
But darling I won't die
As long as you're ok

DON'T THINK THAT I DON'T MISS YOU

Don't think that I don't miss you.
I cry when I'm alone.
The only time I kiss you are pictures on my phone.
So when the night is over,
And everyone's gone home,
Don't think that I don't miss you.
I only cry alone.

I miss your sense of humor.
I miss your silly grin.
I miss the way you held me and all that might have been.
But when our home is crowded, with family, friend or foe,
I do not shed a tear, nor bow my head too low.

But don't think I don't miss you. I cry myself to sleep.
I pet the dog once hated and full of sorrows weep.
I watch her as she waits outside. She lingers at the drive. She
hopes you're coming home soon. She thinks you're still alive.

So don't think I don't miss you. We're staring out the door. We
wonder if you see us on some celestial shore.
So don't think I don't miss you.
I'll see you by and by.
Our meeting will be heavenly and there with you I'll cry.

GOOD GRIEF

Put one foot in front of the other
Find some time to call your mother
Feeling sad, call your dad
Need a laugh, call your brother
Put one foot in front of the other.

Good grief
Lists to keep
Great loss
T's to cross

Good grief
Brush your teeth
Great loss
Better floss

Grin and bear it
With friends share it
Cry a while
Until you smile

Good grief
Wash your sheets
Great loss
Mattress toss

Good grief
Floors to sweep
Great loss
Heavy cross

Say you're fine
Glass of wine
Wipe your tear
Mug of beer

Put one foot in front of the other
Find some time to call your mother
Feeling sad, call your dad
Need a laugh, call your brother
Put one foot in front of the other.

MY DAUGHTERS

Today I realized that my daughters are saving me.
Saving me from sadness.
Saving me from loneliness.
My daughters have come together in unity. They plan days for me. They plan outings for me. They take turns being with me. They spend the night with me, as if they have no families of their own. They are here for me.
In their own grief they comfort me. What more could I ask of them. They have outdone all the other daughters in the world. In my mind, there are no better children who have ever existed or ever will. These daughters of mine, who can compare. No one. Not one.

GOOD SHEETS AND PICKLED BEETS

Give me good sheets and pickled beets.
My shopping list is full.
Laying here it's crystal clear my budget takes no bull.

I'm off the booze and have to choose brown eggs or toilet
paper.
My pay check laughs and mocks my job.
I'm dreaming up some caper.

If robbery is now my speed, I'll need to chug more wine.
But I can't buy a Chardonnay unless you'll spare a dime.

Good sheets, pickled beets with cottage cheese galore.
But can't afford that lumpy goo unless I play the whore.

So give me sleep on cotton sheets and coffee when I wake up.
I'll dine for cheap on pickled beets and coupon cutting take up.

JUST YOU AND ME

The whole world is on fire.
But here, it's just you and me.
Syria has fallen and Turkey is in ruins.
But here, it's just you and me.
Mary at your right and Joseph at your left.
Here, it's just you and me.
A crucifix and a monstrance.
Jesus, fastened to both.
I stare at two who are one.
Here, it's just you and me.
There is a spell of silence cast over me.
Unspoken words find rest in a lover's gaze.
Here, it's just you and me.

IT'S NOT SUICIDE I LONG FOR

It's not suicide I long for
Just a way to ease the pain
When my prayers go unanswered
Though the wick be set aflame

When the flickering of the candle
Seems to mock my guilt and shame
When the night of grief and terror
Gives its blessing then refrain

Surely death will come at twilight
My horizons not yet gray
But the darkness of my longing
Begs one sun drenched golden ray

Do not watch me in dark corners
Gleaming sickle shining bright
For I will not draw you hither
You are ghastly in my sight

No the death I long for daily
Is a way to ease my pain
But if suicide the answer
Then my loss will be no gain

So death put down your sickle
I do not wish to play
I will cast the midnight reaper
On the flame that lights my way

Now I wait until my Father
At the doorstep calls for me
There's no easy way to Heaven
Or the One who sets me free

It's not suicide I long for
Just a way to ease the pain
When my prayers go unanswered
Though the wick be set aflame

MY SOUL LOST ITS HOME

Six months ago, my soul lost its home.
Widowed too soon,
I've started to roam.
Once in a while I feel like I'm home.
But roads become highways and highways ain't home.

FATHER'S DAY

We've had many firsts without your dad.
First Christmas came quickly.
First New Year
First Valentine's
Katie's first birthday without him.
Now it's Father's Day.
It may be the hardest holiday so far. Because it's for and about him. And we are without him.
But to me, it's the first holiday with the most light and the most love because this Father's Day we see him as he truly is.
We see his kindness.
We see his love.
We see his impact on all of us.
We see so many who loved him.
We see his strength.
We see his courage.
We see his true worth.
We see his genius.
We see his understanding.
We see his gentleness.
It's the hardest but it's the best, because the veil is lifted.
We see inside and underneath and beyond.
We see what he left us.
A legacy of love and protection and paternity done right.
I miss him. I know you do too. Words don't cut it. We have a broken heart that only fond memories can mend. He was so great. Now no one can miss that. Now, it's so blatantly obvious.

Now is the Father's Day to remember him. And in doing so, may your broken hearts be mended, even if only a little bit. We give him the gift of our sadness and love and our gratefulness. He gives us the gift of eternal love and unceasing devotion. He is with us even now. It is still his Father's Day.
I love you, more than words can express.

24 WEEKS

24 weeks and I can't quit from cryin.
All I remember is,
"Jeannie, am I dyin?"

Last words, "I love you," but I didn't hear.
Room full of family.
Room full of fear.

They on his left,
I on his right.
Four forty four when he gave up the fight.

24 weeks and I can't stop my cryin.
All I remember is, "Jeannie, am I dyin?"

Last breath was short,
Oh was he tryin,
24 weeks but I can't quit from cryin.

HERE I SIT

Here I sit
All a dither
Happy persona starting to wither.
I'm mad as hell and don't know why.
I'd like to scream but start to cry.
Praying helps
Cause God is bigger
But here I sit
All a dither.

ALONE

I am alone
I am alone with the Father
I am alone with the Son
I am alone with the Holy Spirit
I am alone with the Blessed Mother
I am alone with St Joseph
I am alone with all the saints
I am alone with David
I am never alone.

BROKEN HEART

Please heal Gavin's broken heart.
From you let him not depart.

Please heal Addison's broken heart.
From you let her not depart.

Please heal Kayden's broken heart.
From you let her not depart.

Please heal Micah's broken heart.
From you let him not depart.

In their sorrow,
In their pain,
Heal their hearts to trust again.

Let them know the thrill of laughter.
Let them feel the joys of love.
Keep them for your ever after.
Keep them for your home above.

38 YEARS

He remembered dates and numbers and counted the years by what car he drove. "It was 1985, remember? You drove the brown Cutlass and I drove the Formula Ford." He never mentioned his daily driver, just the race car. And he always remembered our anniversary. We didn't always give gifts, but we always went out to eat and I got a funny card with his signature smiley face drawn on it. It always said, " I'll love you forever." And he did.

When asked when we got married, I had to think (as I just did) before saying June or July. I recalled it was the same month as his birthday, so July. Then I would say the 25th with a question mark at the end. He would laugh and say, "No, the 20th." I already knew the 1985 part. He had made that number a part of my email address when we set it up years ago. On July 20, 1985, we said, "I do." And I still do.

WHY AM I OK

I'm ok because we were happy.
I'm ok because there was nothing left unsaid.
I'm ok because I believe in eternity.
I'm ok because I had true love.
I'm ok because David was a really good husband.
I'm ok because I had retired the year before and we spent every day together.
I'm ok because I don't remember the last fight we had.
I'm ok because he left me financially secure.
I'm ok because I have a home.
I'm ok because I have kids.
I'm ok because my daughters love me.
I'm ok because my daughters have spent days and weeks with me since he died.
I'm ok because my girls adored their father.
I'm ok because I have friends.
I'm ok because Jesus has prepared me for this time.
I'm ok because Jesus loves us.
I'm ok because the sun is shining and the clouds float by on a blue sky.
I'm ok because I have music.
I'm ok because my darling grandchildren will visit me this weekend.
I'm ok because I can go to church and pray any time I want to.
I'm ok because David and I had a good life together.
I'm ok because I have loved and I have love.

SWING WIDE THE DOOR

I knock and you open.
A thin, tiny crack.
Your solemn face nervous.
You take a step back.

Eyes fearful and darting.
There's so much to lose.
You calculate options.
There's much now to choose.

Swing wide the door.
Let Me come in.
There's nothing to fear here.
Except for your sin.

The door opens slowly
A bit more you see.
But still not enough
To truly see Me.

My yoke, it is easy.
My burden is light.
You glance back not trusting
About to take flight.

Swing wide the door.
Forget what has been.
There's joy everlasting
Just give up your sin.

Swing wide the door.
You'll like what's in store.
You'll see all My glory
And love evermore.

The door inches open.
Your form now I see.
You're nervous and glitchy
So fearful of Me.

I smile your direction
I open my arms.
My eyes meet your gaze.
But sense your alarm.

Swing wide your arms now.
Just don't turn away.
I promise to love you.
For each passing day.

Nothing can part us
Except your command.
Please let me love you
As God and as man.

Swing wide the door.
Embrace all I am
I promise to love you
As God and as man.

A HUNGRY DOG

When worry follows me around like a hungry dog,
Surrender feeds him.

When sadness follows me around like a hungry dog,
Surrender feeds him.

When fear follows me around like a hungry dog,
Surrender feeds him.

Surrender, like nothing else, relieves the pain of living and loving in a world that doesn't always make sense.

Surrender, like no other tonic, relieves the pain of not knowing the end of much of anything.

Surrender, to the God who created the universe is better than surrender to the universe.

The universe doesn't love me, though it sustains me. The universe didn't die for me, though it lives for me. The universe doesn't know me like God knows me. It is incapable of loving, dying, knowing though it is capable of giving. But surrender is a gift from a loving, dying, knowing God.

When doubt follows me around like a hungry dog,
Surrender feeds him.

When yearning follows me around like a hungry dog,
Surrender feeds him.

When loss follows me around like a hungry dog,
Surrender feeds him.

What I didn't know, I now know. What I didn't feel, I now feel.
What I didn't see, I now see.
That life is not, and was never, under my control.
That surrender leads to joy.
That surrender leads to peace.
That the abundant life is a surrendered life.

It is a who, not a what, that I surrender to.
It is a who, not a what, that beckons me.
It is a who, not a what, that draws me.

Who but my beloved Jesus, the one who lived and loved and died for me.
Who but the King of Kings and Lord of Lords.
Who but the One who surrendered His throne to give me His crown.
Who but Love and Mercy itself.

It is He who is the hungry dog and He who follows me until I trust Him enough to surrender. It is my surrender that feeds Him and He who feeds me.

IT'S NOT DEATH WE LONG FOR

It's not death we long for
We long for calm
Not a stillness born of nothingness
But a stillness born of fullness and freedom

Freedom from sadness
Freedom from remorse
Freedom from anger
Freedom from desire

Freedom from anxiety
And stress
Freedom from longing
And love unmet

It's not death we long for
So don't walk down that road
It's change and it's freedom
The illusive lighter load

A wise man once told me
My yolk is easy
My burden light
So take up your cross and fight the good fight

But sobs and sadness befall all I do
My burdens are heavy
My triumphs are few

When hopelessness comes
I run to the tree
Upon which my sorrows are cast in the sea

It's not death I long for
It's freedom from me
My plans and my wishes
Surrendered to Thee

NEW DAY

Today is new
The old is gone
The bridegroom is no longer in the household
So now we fast.

We fast to discipline ourselves for a greater work
For the greater good
We fast to atone for our sins
And the sins of our loved ones
Like the athlete we give up pleasure now for the greater glory of an eternal prize.

Not just from food and drink do we fast
Our eyes will not rest on evil
Our ears will not harken to sin.
There is no laughter when folly abounds
For the weight of a soul is in the balance
There can be no joy in Hell.

Keep me from sin all the days of my life
Let the heavenly sacrifices made for me not be for naught.
Let my sacrifices for others not be wanting.
In this new day we may see the beauty of our God
That none shall be lost and joy may be eternal.

Grace is free and Forgiveness without cost but my access to it comes from assent to God.
Do not let us presume that God winks at our disobedience.
If I hold my truth above His, my pride hides His grace
If I choose my will above His, will I later repent?

Joy is what I long for above all happiness.
I will strive for joy, not happiness.
Not as the world does in lust, power and pleasure.
But in thankfulness and worship of my Creator and Savior.

It is a new day.
The old is gone
Now there is no one greater or more loving.
There is no one else alive who lives to love me.

THY WILL

I felt God say to me, "You are trying to calm the storm and give Me the cup to drink. I want to calm the storm while you drink the cup."

"I will say to you, "Peace be still." You must say to Me, "Father, not mine, but Thy will."

MY HEART IS FULL

I love you Jesus;
My heart is full.
I love you Mary;
My home is full.
I love you Joseph;
My life is full.

I love my life today;
My heart is full.
I love my life today;
My home is full.
I love my life today;
My life is full.

In all I do, in all I see, my joy is simply faith, home and family. With these three, my heart is full. With these three my home is full. With these three my life is full.

Jesus, Mary and Joseph are three. Father, Son and Holy Spirit are three. Faith, home and family are three. Three is wholeness. Three is wellness. Three is complete. Today, I am whole. Today, I am well. Today, I am complete. Love comes in threes.

SOMBER CELEBRATION

The celebration somber.
The birthday cake is blue.
The cemetery quiet.
The celebrants are few.

But here your girls remember,
The man who was their friend.
A father to a daughter.
Until the very end.

A husband to a wife as well.
My dreams you made come true.
A comedy of laughter.
Though tragedies we knew.

So thank you for the life you shared.
You gave us gifts untold.
Your legacy eternal,
Now 75 years old.

So happy birthday honey.
We miss you every day.
It's how we've come to realize,
Our best friend went away.

TOPSEY TURVY

Topsey Turvy is God's mercy
Most unworthy
Grace flows free.

Topsey Turvy is God's mercy
Most unworthy
Ransomed be.

Topsey Turvy is God's mercy
Most unworthy
Loved most sweet.

Topsey Turvy is God's mercy
Most unworthy
Praises be.

IF

If there are souls to be saved
Let me pray.
If there is Truth to proclaim
Let me pray.
If there are saints to be made
Let me pray.

Desiring only your good pleasure
Let me love souls without measure.

Whatever you want of me.
Whatever you need of me.
Let me live my life for love of Thee.

BATHE ME IN YOUR MERCY

Bathe me in Your mercy
Wash me white as snow
Open up the heavens
Let Your graces flow.

Come to me in quiet
Still my heart to pray
Teach me to surrender
Lead me in Your way.

Stir my heart at daybreak
Fix my gaze above
Hand in hand with Mary
Tread this walk of love.

Calm my heart at midnight
Fix my gaze on You
Three o'clock surrender
Mercies through and through.

Bathe me in Your mercy
Wash me white as snow
Open up the heavens
Let Your graces flow.

GOD'S REALM

God's realm is a tearful widow giving thanks for 37 happy years of marriage.

God's realm is a lonely widow taking comfort in her three daughters.

God's realm is a tired widow giving thanks that she can eat yogurt for dinner.

God's realm meshes sorrow with joy and death with everlasting life. God's realm is upside down, inside out, topsy turvy.

God's realm is a bored widow lounging in a library without a care in the world.

God's realm is a dutiful widow going home to feed a dog that misses her husband as much as she does.

God's realm is a yearning widow who is too young to live alone but too old to start over.

God's realm is ever changing. He will lead me, though I have no idea where. He simply says, "Come and see." So I come. Because I truly want to see.

IF I WERE TO MARRY

If I were to marry, I'd marry rich.
I'd have a masseuse and a chef on a yacht as we sailed around the world.
But if I were not to marry, I'd go from monastery to monastery eating monks' bread and drinking monks' coffee.
When you can do anything, your mind tends to wander. And so I will wander until I find my new home.

WRINKLES ON MY FOREHEAD

There's wrinkles on my forehead,
Where freckles used to be.
My eyes are growing smaller,
Dark circles plain to see.

Around my mouth are tiny lines,
Though never did I smoke.
My photos from a year ago,
Seem like a crazy joke.

At 61 a beauty.
At 62 a troll.
The death of my dear husband
Has taken quite a toll.

But looking in the mirror
I see who David loved.
And all those little wrinkles now fit me like a glove.

I'm not ashamed of aging.
Though quickly did it come.
The love and laughter now turned tears is where they've all come from.

So wrinkles on my droopy face,
At home with you I'll be.
For I have lived a lovely life because my love loved me.

LEAD ME

Father Joseph
Mother Mary
Here at adoration tarry.
Linger long enough to lead me
To the cross where I am freed.

Take me by your gentle hand.
Take me to the cross most grand.
Find me sitting at His feet.
Find my soul in rapture sweet.

Lead me where you want to go.
Lead me where I do not know.
Lead me on to joys unseen.
Lead me on to pastures green.

Crowned with thorns in pain He cried.
Lead me to his wounded side.
Lead me to His nail pierced hands.
On His feet His life blood lands.

Let me tarry with your Son.
On the tree, His battle won.
Monstrance crowning all He is.
All my adoration His.

In His sacred heart I'll hide.
Let me be His humble bride.
Mercy deep and treasures wide,
Flowing from His wounded side.

Lead me on to sacred ground.
Lead me on where Christ is found.
Lead me when I want to roam,
Lead me to my Heavenly home.

I LOVE THIS LIFE

I love this life You've given.
I glory in today.
But if it were my choosing,
He'd not have gone away.

The blinds are barely open.
The shade tree view sublime.
I sit upon my half made bed,
And wile away the time.

I conjure him beside me.
He gently takes my hand.
And off we go together,
Into the promised land.

I wonder at his presence.
I ponder his demise.
I make up different outcomes,
And try them on for size.

My life is what it should be.
But lingers still the pain.
I thrill when I imagine,
His hand in mine again.

I love this life You've given.
I glory in today.
But if it were my choosing,
He'd not have gone away.

EPILOGUE

FATHER'S DAY
by Patty McCullough Hale

Just saying I miss you doesn't say enough.
Yet I cannot describe the physical pain in my gut when I remember you are not here.
I cannot explain the laughter when I think of all our shenanigans.
I have trouble expressing the depth of the emptiness in my soul.
How it's possible I still feel how much you love me is beyond comprehension.
But saying I miss you doesn't say enough.
It doesn't explain why I think of you a thousand times in a day.
I struggle to express the random smile when I hear your voice in my head.
It cannot make sense how I still detect your presence.
I don't understand how my heart continues to beat without our daily conversations.
But saying I miss you just doesn't seem to say enough.

MISSING
by Patty McCullough Hale

Missing you.
Missing how easy it was to pick up the phone and call you.
Miss how you were always eager to hear about my latest adventures.
Miss running errands with you.
Miss our road trips to the races.
Miss how you told me I was perfect just the way I am.

I could never have imagined how different life would be without you.
It's too quiet without your laughter.
It's too dull without your unique sense of humor.
It's too empty without your unmistakable presence.
It's lonely at the track.
It's too hard without someone telling me I'm perfect just the way I am.

You believed in me.
You were proud of me.
You encouraged me.
You cheered for me.
You cried with me.
You reminded me I'm perfect just the way I am.

I can only pray I gave back even half of what you gave me.
I pray you enjoyed my company just as much as I enjoyed yours.
I pray I made you laugh.

I pray you knew I was always cheering you on.
I pray I exemplified the wisdom you passed on to me.
I pray you knew I was there to the very end.
I pray you knew you were perfect just the way you were.

I love you. I miss you. I look forward to the day we meet again in Heaven.

TODAY

by Patty McCullough Hale

I want my dad back.
There are days I just can't do life without him.
This is one of those days.
The tears continue to fall and they are harder to hide.
Amazing how I can feel so alone with only one person missing.
Some days I'm fine.
Today is not one of those days.
I feel cast aside and of little value.
Like a little girl lost.
Sometimes I just wanna sleep it all away.
All the while knowing I never would.
There will never be that day.
I need my dad back.
The one who always got me.
I'm so lonely without him.
I'm so sad.
It hurts so much.
How do I come back from it all.
When does the loss become just a normal day.
When does tomorrow become today.

Eulogy by Patty Hale
David's Eldest Daughter

The Bible taught me that with great joy comes great sorrow. So, when friends and family ask how I'm doing, I tell them I am lucky to be this sad.
I affectionately called him Dooda and he always called me Worm. If you know me, then you have endured many stories about my dad. Even at my age, this daddy's girl bragged about how cool and utterly amazing and talented my dad was. Our relationship was unique. Special and irreplaceable to say the least. Next to my hubby and son, Dooda was my favorite person on this planet. Growing up, I thought it was normal to have a race car driver as a dad. It was normal to receive a 50cc Suzuki dirt bike for your 6th birthday; to be driven to school in a dune buggy that your dad built from the ground up. And then there was hanging around the State Fair Coliseum watching the Blackhawks hockey team each week. I do recall the first time I disappointed my dad. Around the age of 7, he gave me the choice of hockey skates or figure skates. I already had the Dorothy Hamill haircut, so I opted for the figure skates. I could tell by the look on his face that my decision made him sad. But...everything turned out fine because after about a month, I begged for those hockey skates. He was happy to oblige, and he even bought me my own hockey stick, which I still have to this day.

In my memory of being a little girl, my dad and I were inseparable. I remember hanging out with him at his job when he worked at BAP (British Auto Parts.) I tagged along to the shop when he and the guys were prepping the cars for the next race. And if the races were local, I was right there at the track with him and my mom. Fast forward several years and not much had changed. Dooda was working for Smiley, and he would occasionally take me to school in a street rod. Then, when it was time, he taught me how to drive, a stick shift of course, which involved a lot of patience on his part. By this time, he had been playing hockey for a while, as a goalie! So, I spent a lot of late nights rink side cheering him on. And now...It's been at least ten years or so that I have been able to attend all of Dooda's races. Some local, some 4-6 hours away. There was never a dull moment on those trips. We filled the miles with jokes, movie quotes, and comparing our aches and pains. Sharing our goals and dreams and of course, critiquing the driving of the others on the road.

The racetrack is my happy place. I loved watching my dad nourish the relationships with all the guys. Some friendships being 45-60 years strong. I would well up with pride when anyone would ask Dooda for advice or help with a repair. I got a kick out of how he always wanted to start his races in the back of the pack. He found it more exciting and challenging to work his way through other drivers to the front rather than starting there to begin with. I hope you racers will still have me. I want to be back at the track even in my dad's absence. I know my dad's legacy will live on through y'all and that will be some much-needed healing for me. I promise to keep making sandwiches and to always have Double Stuffed Oreos.

I will miss Dooda's updates on his latest projects. I found it amusing that he thought I understood him when he described these things in detail to me. And even though I didn't always understand, I found fascinating the things he knew and the things he could do with his hands. I guess I never minded listening because he always had an ear for me.

My sisters were saying that they wanted to record his voicemail so they could hear him when they wanted. Almost at the same time, Kelly and I said we never really heard his voicemail much. The reason being he always answered the phone for his girls when we called. He was and will always be an awesome dad. Jeannie said the other day, "if you girls were going through something, your dad was going through it with you." I know this to be true. My dad has cried with me through heartaches and rejoiced with me through celebrations. Dooda taught me the importance of honesty, loyalty and laughter. I want to be as corny as he was when I grow up. He also passed on his habit of always being early. In this case, I think he went on to Heaven a little too soon. Though it doesn't make it easier, I know when I look at the big picture, I see God has placed all the pieces together perfectly. To quote one of my favorite songs...Because you, God, finish what you start, I will trust you in the process.

I'll close with one of my favorite memories. It fits perfectly inside the hole left in my heart. Around the age of 19, I was playing on the V-Dub Folks softball team with my dad. We were all out warming up when a fellow teammate threw a really fast and really low ball my way. I just missed it with my glove, and it crashed into the front of my ankle. I gasped and began biting my lip to keep from crying. I wanted to be brave for my dad and I sure didn't want to embarrass him by bawling in front of his coworkers. Seeing I was in pain, he ran over to me and walked me to the dugout. He sat me down and calmly said, "It's OK to cry." With those four words, I burst into tears. I am thankful that, in my sweet dad's passing, my family and friends have reminded me that it's OK to cry. The 51 years I had with my Dooda are worth every tear.

Eulogy by Kelly Sparks

David's Youngest Daughter

My dad was the epitome of a good dad. There was never a time when I doubted his love for me. He was genuinely interested in what I was doing and would always find a way to be involved. Whether it was softball in high school or dumpster diving now. He has always been right there, taking me to batting practice or meeting me for breakfast to hear about our recent trash finds. He was always cheering me on and encouraging me to be the best version of myself.

When Alex and I first got married, we decided to move into our van and drive around the country. My dad was worried and did express his thoughts on our decision. But whenever we got back from the trip, he surprised us with a huge map in the game room, marked with pins in every city we had visited. He kept up to date with it over the years and it is something that I will forever cherish. That was just the way my dad was. He was so loving and excited to participate in my life, no matter the adventure. His love and support have guided me in ways that I, even now, may not recognize.

I don't know what life is going to be like without my dad, but I can tell you what the last two weeks have looked like since his passing. And it looks like my sisters being there for my mom, and it looks like my mom, stronger than any of us knew, braving the waves of this heartbreak with courage and resilience. It looks like the whole family weeping and mourning a man we so deeply admired and adored. It looks like a family whose strength, loyalty and perseverance were taught by example.

I would not be the adventurous person I am today if it weren't for my dad encouraging me to try new things, especially

when they scared me. My dad has always been my biggest cheerleader and I will dearly miss getting to share this life with him. I love my dad more than words can express. And I will keep doing my best to make him proud of me.
I love you dad.

Eulogy by Katie Lira

David's Middle Daughter

My earliest memory of my dad is going to the movies to see The Lion King when my mom and little sister were out of town visiting Patty when Micah was a newborn. I felt so cool holding his hand, walking through the mall to the theater. My first of many times at the movies with my dad. The first of many times I remember him making me feel special.

My dad was a present father and absolutely loved being a grandpa. He attended all of Kelly and I's sporting events, school functions and I don't remember there ever being a time in my life where I thought, "My dad isn't around much." He continued that with my kids and watching them play and compete brought him so much joy. We all knew he was funny but not everyone got to see the little ways he showed just how deeply he cared for us, his family. One of the greatest gifts my dad gave us was loving our mom so well. Every morning he would open the blinds for my mom because he knew she loved the sun shining in, he would feed the dog, empty the dishwasher and do the laundry. Each night he would close the blinds, lock the doors, load the dishwasher and turn down mom's side of the bed.

If we mentioned we needed anything, he had it for us the next time we saw him, or sometimes he'd just show up and drop it off for us. My dad was generous. He was so easy to love. Steve, a man who bought a car from him is here today. He and his wife Dawn drove all the way from Wisconsin just to be here. Judy, a waitress from his regular spot is here today. He made friends from of what others would have seen as nothing more than a transaction. His heart was just as big as his personality. He loved hanging out with his ROMEO group...Retired, old men eating out! He would talk on the phone for hours, sometimes without any interruption from the guy on the other end, then hang up and say, "Man that guy talks a lot!" He loved watching Hallmark movies with Kayden, shooting guns and swimming with Gavin, and showing Addison how to build things in the shop and watch her play sports. My dad loved music, everything from Aretha Franklin to Carrie Underwood to, believe it or not, Lady Gaga! Growing up, we always watched American Idol. He always watched America's Got Talent with my kids.

My dad was kind and gentle even when the odds said he likely wouldn't be. He built a home for us on acreage so we could have a carefree childhood even though him, not being a high school graduate, meant statistically, he wouldn't amount to much. They say you don't know what you have till it's gone. Not true for us. We knew just how lucky we were. We had a dad who hugged us, said, "I love you," supported us even when he didn't fully understand what we were doing or why. He loved our mom and joked with our friends.

I'll miss the random phone calls in the middle of the weekday asking, "I'm at Wally World. You need anything?"
I'll miss hearing, "King of the Hill's on!" being shouted from the game room.
I'll miss how ridiculously loud he slurped his coffee.
I'll miss going to the movies and him insisting we arrive 30 minutes before it starts even though he'd already reserved seats online.
I'll miss him coming in from the shop smelling of oil and metal.
I'll miss seeing him type with one finger.
I'll miss flinching when he'd walk by as I prepared to be poked in the ribs.

I'll miss curling up in his lap, even now as an adult, and laying my head on his collarbone which always stuck out funny due to it being broken many years ago.
I'll miss him cutting spaghetti louder than anyone would think possible.
I'll miss hearing, "Hi, Mrs. Boo," whenever I came to visit.
I'll miss watching him with my kids. They were so lucky to have him as their Grampies but I hate that their time with him was cut short. He adored them and would have been so thrilled to attend high school graduation, weddings and more sporting events.

My dad was such an incredible man. I'm so grateful to have had him as my dad. He is missed deeply, and we will continue to miss him. He would have loved seeing you all here today. He would have hated the getting dressed up fancy part, but he would have loved seeing my mom looking so beautiful and having so many people he loved all around.

In closing, my dad was never shy about what he wanted at his funeral. He wanted one of his grandchildren to sing Amazing Grace. So, in keeping with that wish, my daughter Addison is going to do just that.

Eulogy by Kayden Lira

David's Eldest Granddaughter, Age 15

I don't know what to say. It hasn't fully hit me yet. I don't quite know when it will. I have so many great memories with you. Watching you fix the golfcart. Laying out by the pool. You getting pecan pie for us to share. Getting annoyed when Addison and I would eat the Zebra cakes from the pantry. Always watching stupid Hallmark movies with those predictable endings, happily ever afters.

I remember once when I asked you what your dream always was and you said, "I lived my dream when I married Nanny." The way you talked about her always made me smile. I loved seeing y'all on the front porch every morning with your coffee. Y'all holding hands while watching TV. Thank you for always recording America's Got Talent for me so we could watch it next time we were together.

All the great memories I'll never forget. One of my favorites is you teaching me to drive the golf cart. I hope someday I will find someone to love me the way you loved Nanny. We will miss you so much. We love you. Fly High.

Eulogy by Addison Lira

David's Youngest Granddaughter, Age 12

First of all, I'd like to thank everyone for coming here today, it means a lot. Before I sing, I'd like to say a few words. It still hasn't hit me that he isn't coming back, that I'm never going to get another disgustingly loud nose blow or airplane snore, no more race car fixing, no more jokes or hugs and no more terrible off-key singing. But I know that this is what he would have wanted, to have all the people he loved here for him, and I also know he would have wanted me to sing for him and so that is exactly what I am going to do.

[Singing]

AMAZING GRACE

Amazing Grace how sweet the sound
That saved a wretch like me.
I once was lost, but now I'm found
Was blind but now I see.

Twas grace that taught my heart to fear
And grace my fears relieved.
How precious did that grace appear
The hour I first believed.

Through many dangers, toils and snares
I have already come.
Tis grace that brought me safe thus far
And grace will lead me home.

When we've been there ten thousand years,
Bright shining as the sun.
We've no less days to sing God's praise
Than when we've first begun.

Amazing grace how sweet the sound
That saved a wretch like me.
I once was lost, but now I'm found
Was blind but now I see.

Made in the USA
Columbia, SC
08 October 2024

7cc57dc7-be57-428e-8278-36c794a52066R01